ABANDONED
NORTHERN VIRGINIA

ABANDONED NORTHERN VIRGINIA

IN THE SHADOW OF THE NATION'S CAPITAL

LIZ ROLL

AMERICA THROUGH TIME®
ADDING COLOR TO AMERICAN HISTORY

This book is dedicated to my DCUE friends, and especially Andrew Straatveit, Cindy Vasko, and Eric Brown, who give me unwavering support and friendship

America Through Time is an imprint of Fonthill Media LLC
www.through-time.com
office@through-time.com

Published by Arcadia Publishing by arrangement with Fonthill Media LLC
For all general information, please contact Arcadia Publishing:
Telephone: 843-853-2070
Fax: 843-853-0044
E-mail: sales@arcadiapublishing.com
For customer service and orders:
Toll-Free 1-888-313-2665

www.arcadiapublishing.com

First published 2019

ISBN 978-1-63499-185-8

Typeset in Trade Gothic 10pt on 15pt
Printed and bound in England

CONTENTS

INTRODUCTION

> *... most writers, and most other artists, too, are primarily motivated in their desperate vocation by a desire to find and to separate truth from the complex of lies and evasions they live in, and I think that this impulse is what makes their work not so much a profession as a vocation, a true calling.*
>
> Tennessee Williams
> *A Streetcar Named Desire*

There is something fascinating about nature reclaiming her turf: vines climbing bricks, pulling the mortar out; trees growing through cracks in the cement; and tendrils curling around, covering the windows. Wind blows through the fissures in the bricks, and evidence of campfires, graffiti, and other interlopers is all around. Abandoned buildings give me a chill, but also a sense of peace. They are harboring secrets that we mortals will never know of. The walls keep their secrets well—even an expert researcher could never know everything that went on in a place to make it become abandoned. We can try to understand, visit the space, investigate, but we can never be certain. The emotions live in the walls: the tears when the door was closed for the last time, the laughter that was shared before things went wrong, and, often, the blood, sweat, and tears that went into making the place more than a place, but a home, church, school, or business. Such is the lure of exploring—to gain access to these emotions, and photograph a place and create something lovely and beautiful, and realize that Mother Nature is reclaiming the place for Herself.

1

ABANDONED HOUSES

When I was a kid, about five or six years old, my mom, brother, and I decided to go into an abandoned house in New Hampshire. As I stood agape taking in the king-size dining room table and chairs, downed electric wire across the room, and an honest-to-God cartoon-like arch of a mouse hole, I wondered, and have often since, why one would abandon a perfectly good home? Let it go, leave everything behind, waste all that money, let it go back to nature?

Apparently, there are a lot of reasons, because abandoned houses are a common sight, even in affluent Northern Virginia.

The biggest reason people abandon their homes is often financial difficulties—it is almost always about the money. Divorce and death are also major reasons. Take divorce first: a couple will split, and the one left with the house finds out soon enough that he or she cannot afford to keep it. The bank may foreclose or the person may just walk away, vowing to start a new life elsewhere. The other common reason houses become abandoned is death in the family. When people die without a will, all sorts of nasty things can happen. Relatives come out of the woodwork, and fighting ensues. Meanwhile, the property falls into disrepair. Perhaps they have not paid the property tax, and the municipality takes the home. Or maybe they have decided to rent it out, and the renters destroy it. Sometimes, the expenses just get to be more than the house is worth, but the house stays, ripe for vandals, squatters, and poachers.

Also consider the family farm. Small family farms are dependent on family dynamics—and the same rules apply. If there is death or divorce, the farm will suffer. With the prestige of farming on the decline, the children of farmers may not be interested in taking over the family farm. Many cannot afford to take over the farm, even when the desire exists. Big agriculture and farm consolidation are destroying small rural communities and littering the landscape with abandoned homes that must be torn down. Many of these houses are more than 100 years old.

Two-thirds of the counties in Iowa, almost all of them rural, have seen their populations decline since 2010, according to the U.S. census. Houses in the Midwestern United States number in the thousands and were built in a style called Corn Belt Cube. Space was maximized and style was limited. Some of these structures will qualify as historic properties, and most will either be torn down or left to rot. Often, the houses are torn down to get them off the property tax rolls. The ones that do not get demolished are often for sentimental reasons, older parents hoping their kids will settle down in the old homestead.

All of these reasons, and so many more, for houses left to the elements, yet I still find it very sad and wonder why anyone would abandon a perfectly good home.

This house is typical of what one might find in rural Virginia.

It is almost as if the residents just stepped out for a carton of milk and never returned.

Above: Natural disasters account for many abandoned houses. New Orleans is rife with houses still marked, fourteen years later, with large X's placed there after Hurricane Katrina devastated the city in 2005.

Left: The cost of letting a house rot is less than the cost of demolition, especially in rural areas.

Above: Sometimes a house will be inherited, and the heir is not local or cannot sell the house.

Right: A lampshade blows in the breeze.

A bed in rural Virginia awaits its occupant.

It appears that this family was packed and ready to go, then just vanished without a trace.

Quite often, pianos are present in abandoned homes; the reason is simple: this was their main form of entertainment.

Found in a home in Northern Virginia.

Above left: A toy is left behind in an abandoned home in Winchester, VA.

Above right: It is a little spooky to find peoples' clothing in abandoned homes; it still makes me wonder what happened to them and why they left.

Below: According to the current owner of this house, the proprietor of the Alberene Soapstone Company in Schuyler, VA, owned and lived in this house. It is also known locally as The Company House. The house is on private property.

The exterior of this house uses soapstone around the first floor from the Alberene Soapstone Company. The soapstone is still quite visible, even though the house has been abandoned for quite some time. The soapstone quarry opened in 1883 and is the only one in the country that remains. The vein that Alberene uses to mine is one of the largest soapstone seams in the world, and can be 300 to 400 million years old. Contrary to popular belief, soapstone is as hard as granite or stone, and is used for countertops, heated floors, pavers, and the like, and is environmentally friendly.

The Adam Rader Plantation House near Timberville, Virginia, was a very unusual home, as it had a half-basement, two floors of living space, and a large attic. It was built near a small stream for easy water usage. The rill may have run through the basement at some point, which could have been used as refrigeration for food stored there. Built of giant logs, chimneys flanked either side. There was reportedly large room on the second floor that is believed to have been a meeting room for church activities since there were no Reformed churches in the area at that time.

Adam Rader and his wife, Margaret, were Lutheran missionaries who founded the Rader Church in Timberville.

The remains of the Adam Rader house, *circa* 1744. The ruins are now on private property in Timberville, VA. The house continues to deteriorate; soon there will be nothing left of this historic home. The original parcel of land was about 100 acres.

Adam Rader and his brother-in-law, Alexander Painter, donated 3 acres for the church in 1765. The original building is long gone; the current church was built in 1965.

It is believed that Adam Rader and his family are buried on a hill near the house, not at this church cemetery.

Left: The stone marker reads: "May 20th, 1765 Adam Reider and Alexander Painter for the glory of God and the spreading of His precious gospel have given a small quantity of land for the building of a church house to worship God forever as long as the sun shines and the water runs to promote peace and love. Adam Reider Ann Reider Alexander Painter Margaret Painter."

Below: A photo of the original Rader house graces a wall in a friend's farmhouse that occupies the same parcel of property.

2

CHAPMAN-BEVERLEY MILL

Driving at a decent clip west on Interstate 66, one might miss the shell of a building past the exit for Route 15 that is the Chapman-Beverley Mill. The county lines of Prince William and Fauquier pass directly through this gristmill, which is about 40 miles west of Washington, D.C. Father and son Jonathan and Nathaniel Chapman erected the mill in 1742 on the banks of Broad Run, and the family milled cornmeal and flour until 1946. There are also ruins of a family house and graveyard on the site. A fire left the mill in ruins in 1998, but some non-profit groups are attempting to stabilize and preserve it.

The south wall stands seven stories high, and Chapman-Beverley Mill is believed to be the tallest stacked stone building in the United States. No mortar is used in this type of construction; well-placed keystones ensure its stability

The mill originally served local farmers who wanted to process and transfer their crops to the port of Alexandria for exporting to Europe and South America. Already a successful gristmill, business only improved when the Manassas Gap Railroad was completed in 1852, which ran next to the mill, making shipments to Alexandria even faster and simpler.

During the Civil War, the mill was used to cure meats for the Confederate soldiers. When their Union foes advanced too close, the Confederates burned the mill down and charred the meat. About ten years later, the mill was restored and run by the Beverley family. It then changed hands several times until 1903 when it was sold to Charles Furr, who added a general store. The Mill Store operated long after the mill was closed, first as a convenience store and then as a post office.

This photo shows the south wall of Chapman-Beverley Mill. This mill is believed to be the tallest stone stacked structure in the United States. A load-bearing facade stabilizes a stone stacked structure; no mortar is used in this type of construction.

A detail of the fireplace inside the mill.

Chapman-Beverley Mill as seen from the west.

During the Civil War, the Union Army occupied the area near the mill called Thoroughfare Gap; the mill was used by the Confederates as a fortress when they were in the area.

The Manassas Gap Railroad was completed in 1852 and thus made shipments to the Port of Alexandria easier and faster.

3

LAZY SUSAN DINNER THEATRE

Imagine your belly is full of chicken, pasta, and pierogies, you have just downed your third Martini, and you feel pretty good. The lights go down, and the Overture to "Big River" starts. What you have just experienced is classic supper club fare.

Supper clubs were all the rage in the 1930s and 1940s. A kind of social club, where one could get all their evening needs satisfied with one-stop shopping—food, drink, and entertainment, usually a show or music and dancing. They were considered classy joints—folded cloth napkins and a white tablecloth, maybe a candle on the table. As an offshoot of the Prohibition era of speakeasies, people could go and drink legally because the venue was private.

Lazy Susan Dinner Theatre, in Lorton, Virginia, was one such supper club, though not private. They served a Pennsylvania-Dutch buffet and put on a big show in the spring and fall and a smaller show in the summer. At the beginning of the season, they hosted an Agatha Christie murder mystery. The Lazy Susan attracted young aspiring actors (who also waited tables) who might one day land on Broadway. It was one of the first of its kind in the Washington, D.C., area. The supper club theme was added to the restaurant in the 1970s, and it closed forever in 2013.

Roadhouses, the precursor to supper clubs, got their start in the Midwest during Prohibition. Prohibition ran from 1920 until 1933, when the Twenty-first Amendment to the Constitution repealed it. Speakeasies at that time numbered in the thousands.

Lawrence Frank opened the first supper club in Beverly Hills, California. $1.25 would buy a meal of prime rib, baked potato, salad, and Yorkshire pudding.

Wisconsin was the true birthplace of the supper club. Though Lawrence Frank's restaurant was in California, he was a Wisconsin native.

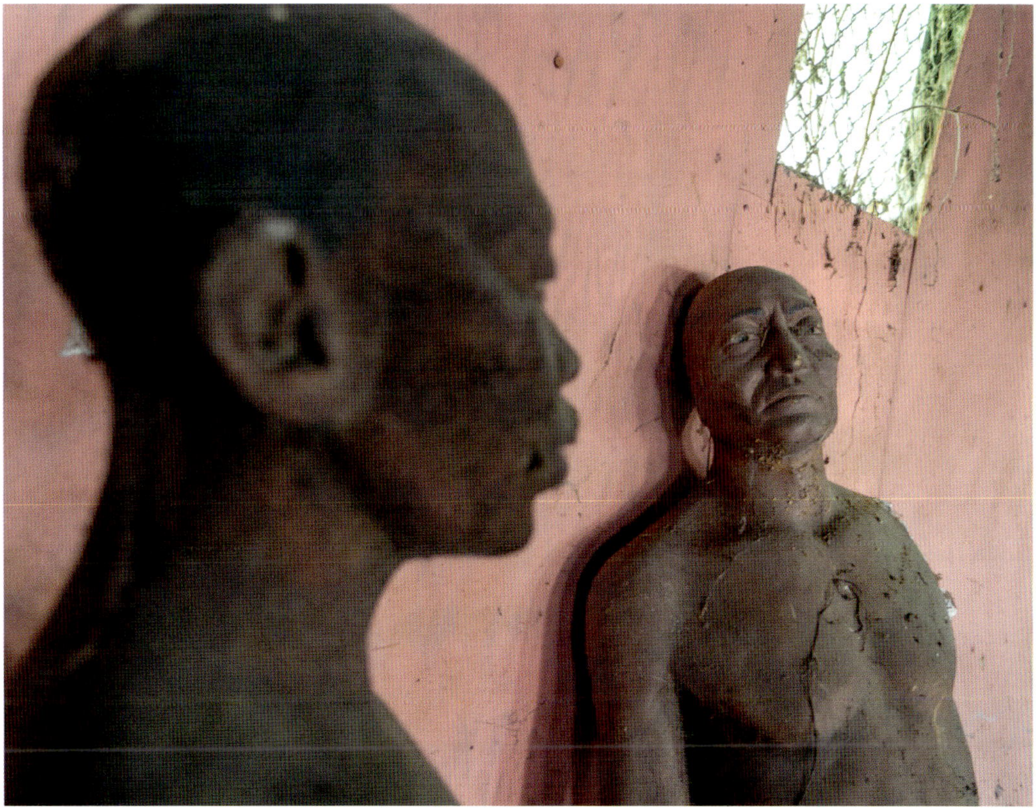

In the beginning, some supper clubs were private, only known to a select few.

Above: Generally more elaborate than speakeasies, supper clubs flourished in many cities and small towns across the country.

Below left: Supper clubs were trendy in the 1930s and 1940s during the Big Band era; on any given night, one might see a surprise performance by Louis Armstrong or Jimmy Dorsey.

Below right: Some establishments offer family-style dining as well as the more typical booth or table setting. Kitsch décor is a staple at some, while others might prefer a bit of taxidermy in the mix.

Above: Some establishments were for adults only, while others catered to families. Most current supper clubs are now children-friendly.

Right: Famous supper clubs include New York's Rainbow Room and the Copacabana.

Meals are generally elaborate and fresh. Home-style cooking seems to be key to the success of the place.

Unlike chain restaurants, each supper club has a unique flavor in entertainment, food, décor, and ambiance.

Above left. The Lazy Susan in Lorton, Virginia, had a small statuary garden at the entrance to the club.

Above right: A small pool greeted guests once inside the supper club, more statues such as this (now) headless monk surrounded them.

Some of the lighting setups backstage at the Lazy Susan.

Above: Prices were fairly reasonable at the time of Lazy Susan's closing: $41.95 for adults Tuesday through Friday and on Sunday, and $44.95 on Saturday. Youths aged eleven to fifteen cost $35 per meal and children aged ten and under cost $25 per meal. The price of admission included dinner (with tea or coffee), show, and tax. Drinks were extra.

Left: Lazy Susan's Facebook page noted on October 17, 2013: "Thank you one and all for taking the time to visit our Facebook page. At this time, The Lazy Susan Dinner Theatre is on hiatus until further notice. We fervently hope to come back again to bring you more shows in the future, but none are scheduled at this time. When the next show finally is in production, we will announce it here, as well as on our website. Please feel encouraged and invited to check out our page here from time to time, as well as our webpage http://www.LazySusan.com. Thank you, one and all, for your continued support of The Lazy Susan Dinner Theatre."

4

FOAMHENGE

What is better than going all the way over to Wiltshire, England, to see a bunch of rocks standing in a circle? Why, having one right here in Virginia you can go to, of course. Foamhenge is exactly what it sounds like: a life-size Styrofoam replica of ancient Stonehenge. Artist Mark Cline erected the creation as an April Fools' Day prank in 2004. Foamhenge was located in Natural Bridge, VA, until September 2016. A new state park forced Cline to sell Foamhenge. It is now located in at Cox Farms in Clifton, VA. It is on private property, and access is extremely limited.

Quite the character, Mark Cline is both a local and international legend and artist. He is the master of sculpting fiberglass into huge roadside attractions that are wildly popular. Cline is quoted in Roadside America as saying of Foamhenge: "I walked into a place called Insulated Business Systems where they make these huge sixteen-foot-tall blocks. As soon as I saw them I immediately thought of the idea: 'Foamhenge.' It took a while for the opportunity to present itself, of course."

Cline is famous for his April Fools' pranks; every year since 2001, a local spot near Cline's workshop in Virginia will be the lucky recipient of one of Cline's masterpieces. One example: in the town of Buena Vista, VA, Cline placed large fiberglass bugs on buildings and public spots along Magnolia Avenue. His creations usually stay put for several months before being removed. In case you are wondering, yes, Foamhenge is astronomically correct.

A sign on an informational "stone" at Foamhenge reads: "Stonehenge took 1500 years to complete using stones weighing as much as fifty tons. An estimated 600–1000 men dragged the stones from Marlborough Downs, twenty miles north. Perhaps used as a temple, observatory, or tomb. Foamhenge was completed in six weeks using beaded Styrofoam blocks weighing up to 420 pounds delivered on four tractor trips from Winchester VA. It took four-five Mexicans and one crazy white man to construct. It's [*sic.*] purpose is to educate and entertain."—M. Cline

Thanks to its proximity to Natural Bridge, Foamhenge received plenty of visitors during its time at this site.

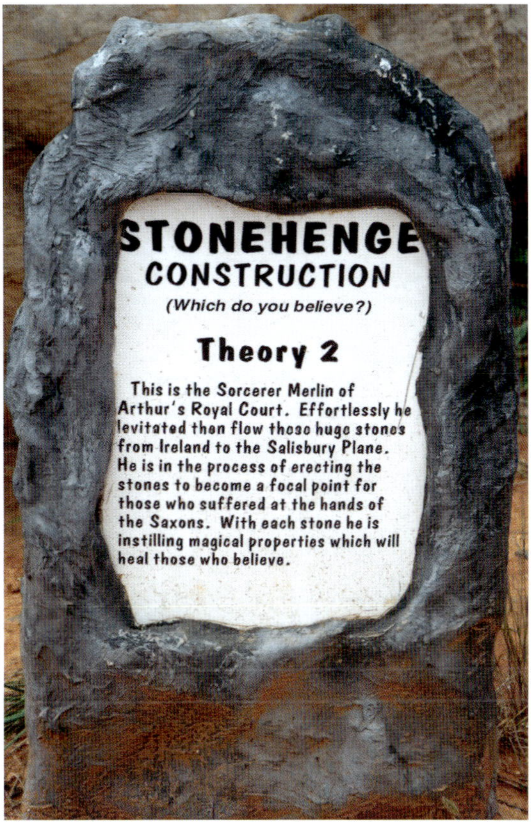

Right: An informational “stone” describes one of Mark Cline’s theories of the construction of Stonehenge.

Below: The proportions of Foamhenge were measured carefully and are accurate.

Above left: A depiction of one theory of how Stonehenge was built: the stone was set standing up using ropes, logs, and leverage.

Above right: A nearby sign reads: "Merlin was cast from a mold created directly from the face of Jamie Jordan in Waynesboro, VA on February 17, 2007 two days after his death, just shy of his sixtieth birthday. It was his request to have me create a lasting impression of him and use it appropriately as he was a big fan of my work. Jamie now lives on as a part of it."—Mark Cline

5

SELMA MANSION

It is not often that abandoned places have a happy ending. Selma Mansion is one such place.

Located high on a hill, Selma Mansion was a typical southern plantation, complete with slaves on about 10,000 acres. They grew corn, rye, oats, and buckwheat. Originally, Thomas Fairfax, 6th Lord Fairfax of Cameron, owned the land, until 1741 when Ann Stevens Thomson Mason acquired the property. Armistead Thompson Mason, who was the grandnephew of George Mason of Virginia fame and a U.S. Senator, built the mansion in 1815. Armistead Mason married Charlotte Eliza Taylor in 1817. He was summarily killed two years later when he and his cousin, Colonel John Mason McCarty, got into a political argument and had a duel to settle the dispute. When Charlotte passed in 1846, the property was left to their only child, a twenty-one-year-old son named Stevens Thomson Mason, Jr.

Most of Selma burned down in the 1890s; only a summer kitchen was spared. The property was later bought and rebuilt by American banker Elijah B. White. The splendid new structure was built in the Colonial Revival style and spared no expense in the name of opulence. The new twenty-room house featured one of America's first intercom systems, an elevator, even a spigot in Mr. White's billiard room that was connected directly to the local springs. Several generations of the White family called Selma home.

The mansion changed hands a number of times until it stood empty in the early 2000s after a Dutch businessman effectively abandoned the property. In 2009, Selma was granted a place on Virginia's most endangered historic sites. This designation opened up a small amount of money to repair the leaky roof and preserve the structural integrity of the 19,000-square-foot building.

In 2016, at a hefty price tag of $1.2 million, Miller and Sharon Virts bought the decrepit Selma from the businessman, and in just two short years, they restored its former magnificence at a cost of roughly $5 million. Experts and master craftsmen were hired, Italian marble was procured, Murano chandeliers were purchased, custom wallpaper was designed, murals were painted, and sconces and fireplace tiles reused. Gardens were planted. A copper roof was installed on the new pool house, with eighteen Corinthian columns used throughout. Authentic materials were used whenever possible. Rooms were redesigned from the original 1900 architectural plans Elijah White had drawn up at the noteworthy Richmond firm of Noland and Baskervill (now known as Baskervill).

Selma Mansion is a true work of art, and I am so pleased that such loving hands could save this mansion. This grand home sits on occupied private property; curiosity seekers should steer clear.

Selma Mansion has had a new infusion of love in the last few years and is now nearly fully restored.

An exterior infrared photo of Selma in 2013.

Originally, Thomas Fairfax, 6th Lord Fairfax of Cameron, owned the 100 acres that Selma Mansion is situated on. In 1741, Ann Stevens Thomson Mason acquired the property.

In January 1818, Armistead Mason put out an advertisement in the local papers to locate a missing slave by the name of "Joe". "His color is a very dark mullato [*sic.*] approaching nearly or quite to a black—he is five feet 8 or 9 inches high; stoops in the shoulders, is of thin visage and habit of body; has a downcast look and stammers in his speech." There was up to a $200 reward.

Another slave, Hanson, "Calling himself Hanson Bouges," ran away on the evening of June 8, 1820. He had a speech impediment: "He brought a fur hat, (nearly new), a fine yellow striped seersucker coat, and a pair of new shoes. Also, on the same night, a likely black nergo [*sic.*] named Ann, about twenty six years of age, upwards of five feet high." It was believed they were heading towards Pennsylvania.

"Major Buoy, well-made and handsome about twenty seven, with considerable cunning", also disappeared that evening. "He took with him a fine brown cloth coat and a green hand-made bottle of linsey do [a handmade bottle-green linen-wool blend coat], and a fine fur hat."

Mary Mason reported a runaway slave on September 10, 1822 from Selma. Adam ran away on the night of August 31 with three other salves from a neighboring plantation. Adam was "fully six feet high, articulates slowly but very distinctly; remarkably erect in his carriage." The reward was $50.

A quote from Selma's Facebook page says this about the new library: "The custom bookcases and shelving are made from Hickory while the mantle is pecan that was procured from a tree harvested a few years ago at George Washington's Mt. Vernon."

According to one local, Selma Mansion is haunted. Some years ago, a local fire department crew went there to see if it was a good candidate for a "live burn"—burning it down for training purposes and then razing what was left. The experience they had was apparently quite hair-raising. According to the lore, a young white woman was caught fraternizing with two male slaves. (It is not clear if she was family.) She was caught and killed on the interior balcony, and left for several days as a warning. She and the two male slaves were subsequently burned and buried out back.

Above left: Another version of the story says the husband had been assaulting the female slaves, to "breed his stock." One of the slaves got caught with her hands on him, which was considered "pleasuring" and not acceptable to the wife. The female slave had her hands cut off and was kept inside the house for years until she died. She was buried in an unmarked grave between the house and the barn. As a reference, the only child of Armistead and Charlotte was Stevens Thompson Mason.

Above right: On several occasions over the years, people visiting there would wake up with holes burned in rugs or other furniture that was left too close to the fire at night. Although nobody was awake or around and all the fires had all been put out, this happened as a reminder. In those days, once a small fire ignited, most structures quickly burned to the ground.

Detail of one of the original fixtures in the bathroom.

A shower curtain ring hangs over the original claw foot bathtub, seen in the previous three photos.

Another bathroom still retains the original toilet with its wooden tank.

The property had several outbuildings, including this barn that was used mostly for storage in recent years.

Furniture and other items, such as silver sets, were found in the barn.

A guesthouse on the property was probably used as slave quarters at the time the house was built.

6

CHURCHES

The Church played a significant role in early Virginia. While many businesses and homes are long gone from the landscape, much effort was put into saving and restoring the historic churches.

Originally, the Virginia General Assembly was in charge of church laws, and required all office holders in the commonwealth to be Anglican (Church of England). Virginia law mandated that all Virginians worship in the Anglican Church, and tax dollars supported the Church.

Adoption of the Virginia Statute for Religious Freedom in 1786 ended tax support for the church and thus later paved the way for the U.S. Constitution's First Amendment, separation of church and state. ("Congress shall make no law respecting an establishment of religion, or prohibiting the free exercise thereof"). No longer were Virginians required to be Anglican, they could choose any religion that suited them.

The settlers who came to Virginia from England were more interested in gaining wealth than piety, and their faith was much shallower than their counterparts in New England. However, Virginians seemed intolerant of non-Christian religions, especially Native American religions, and attempted to convert them to Christianity.

Before 1750, few blacks had joined the Christian fold. In the 1600s, some slaves realized they could gain their freedom if they were baptized, but the Virginia General Assembly closed this loophole in 1667. Over the next century, most slave owners and Anglican ministers ignored the spiritual needs of African-Americans.

Many blacks joined the African Methodist Episcopal Church (AME); others became Primitive Baptists. Primitive Baptists, also known as Hard Shell Baptists or Old School Baptists, are conservative Baptists that split from Baptists around 1812, and originated in the southeastern United States. They differ from Southern Baptists in a number of ways. For example, they do not believe in activities such as Sunday school or school for clergy, and there are no musical instruments during the services.

The AME arose out of racism in 1816 and was the first church borne not of doctrine but discrimination. The AME Church represents the first Civil Rights protest by African-Americans.

The plaster used in Fleetwood Church was horsehair, which was in style between 1920 and 1940. Abandoned in 1974, the church is currently being restored. During the Civil War, the Battle of Brandy Station was fought on June 9, 1863, right next to where the church stands today.

Parishioners completed Fleetwood church, a Methodist church in Brandy Station, VA, in 1881. Some say it is haunted; it was featured on the Fairfax County Public Access TV show *The Witching Hour*.

This Primitive Baptist Church was founded in 1897. It is a historic African-American church and has a cemetery in the back with many of the establishing members buried there.

Interior of the Primitive Baptist Church. Churches were used both as social gathering places and locations to form protests and advance civil rights.

The Winston Chapel in Winston, VA, was built in 1909 by Lucien Dade Winston. It is dedicated to his son, Malcolm Boddie Winston, who died in 1906 at the age of twenty-two. Lucien Winston is also the founder and namesake of the town. He and his wife are also buried in this cemetery.

This cemetery, created in 1906 when Malcolm Boddie Winston died, predates the church. Malcolm was the son of the founder of the town. The stone church and the little cemetery still stand today.

7

LORTON PRISON

The Night of Terror" was probably as awful as it sounds. It was one of many atrocities that occurred at Lorton Prison, then known as Occoquan Workhouse. In 1917, thirty-three suffragists led by Lucy Burns had been protesting at the White House to give women the right to vote. (Lucy Burns was the co-founder of the National Woman's Party along with suffragist Alice Paul.) They were arrested and taken to Lorton. They were then subsequently chained and beaten; Alice Paul was stabbed with her picket sign. Lucy Burns was stripped naked and left in a freezing cell. They spent two weeks at the prison, and while staging a hunger strike, they were force-fed rotten food and endured terrible abuse. News of this incident drew attention to women's suffragist movement and opened the door for investigations into conditions at Lorton and other prisons. Ultimately, 165 suffragists spent time at Lorton. The brutalities that occurred to these women also set the stage for women to finally receive the right to vote in August 1920. The Lucy Burns Museum is being constructed at Lorton to honor these women and commemorate the 100th anniversary of women's right to vote.

President Theodore Roosevelt established Lorton Prison, originally named Occoquan Workhouse and Reformatory, in 1909. The Workhouse, like the Youth Center located about a mile away, was part of the Washington, D.C. corrections system, even though they were situated in Virginia. Originally opened as a farm, or workhouse, for low- to medium-security prisoners, it was an experiment in a new way of prison reform that used fresh air and manual labor for rehabilitation. Ideally, prisoners would come out with skills they did not possess when they went in. In the 1930s, prisoners, using bricks made on site, constructed the buildings. Prisoners also tended to a blacksmith shop, a sawmill, a farm, an orchard, a cannery, and a dairy farm.

A women's workhouse opened on the Lorton complex in 1912, incarcerating women for prostitution, disorderly conduct, or drunkenness. The women oversaw laundry and performed other chores around the prison grounds as they served their sentences.

Lorton Prison has had a rich history of violence and some infamous inmates before it finally closed in 2001. The prison had a reputation for cruel abuse and terrible overcrowding. In July 1986, prisoners set fire to a dozen dorms and forced the evacuation of 800 prisoners. The atmosphere had been tense for days, as the temperature soared and the prison lacked air conditioning.

Towards the end, in the mid- to late 1990s, Lorton resembled nothing like the original farm or the ideal of reform, having added a maximum-security section and solitary confinement that housed some 600 inmates. Budget cuts thinned the guards' ranks and their morale. Crimes committed by guards soared, including taking bribes and smuggling in crack for the prisoners. The last prisoner left at the end of 2001.

Lorton has now become a mixed-use property in highly sought-after Fairfax County. The property now consists of the restored Workhouse Arts Center, homes, apartments, a community cultural arts center, stores, and shops. The Workhouse, opened in 2008, is using the original prison buildings for artist studios and galleries. The studios and galleries give over 100 artists a place to make and show their work at affordable rates. In addition to visual arts, the Workhouse Arts Center is also hosts many of the performing arts. It is well worth a visit.

Left: The Workhouse, also known as the Occoquan Facility, operated as an agricultural work camp, complete with a poultry farm, hog ranch, slaughterhouse, dairy, blacksmith, sawmill, and other structures. Inmates worked on farming the land, as well as producing bricks, manhole covers, retreading tires, and knitting sweaters. A medium-security facility was located on site, but was demolished in 1998.

Below: In 1909, the first inmates, a motley crew of twenty-nine deemed guilty of some petty crime, made the trip on a barge down the Potomac from Washington, D.C., to the banks of the Occoquan, where they lived in tents while they built their own workhouse.

Lorton was known as the prison "without walls," but slowly gained those walls over time. Fences and walls were added in the 1950s.

Conditions at Lorton deteriorated, and overcrowding was the norm.

The maximum-security portion of Lorton was erected in 1931 and had a capacity of 2,066 inmates.

In addition to the maximum-security building, a super-max facility was built at Lorton in 1995. Prisoners were incarcerated in what was called The Hole for twenty-three hours a day. It closed in 2001 along with the rest of the complex.

Right: Supermaxes are known for their strict lockdown policies, lack of amenities, and prisoner isolation techniques. The most violent prisoners are sent to supermaxes. They are used for leaders of criminal organizations and gangs, serial killers, persistent rule breakers, and political prisoners such as terrorists. Prisoners are confined to small cells with no windows up to twenty-three hours a day, and are constantly watched, even though they are isolated. One hour of recreation is offered, in a small cage often referred to as a dog kennel. The incarcerated have no opportunities that will put them in contact with other prisoners, such as mealtime, work, or vocational studies. The cells are soundproof so they cannot even hear one another, and lights stay on twenty-four hours a day. The isolation is total, and escape is deemed impossible.

Below: In the mid-1990s, more than 7,300 prisoners called Lorton home, about 44 percent over what it was intended for.

Above left: In 1986, Lorton experienced major riots and a large fire at the workhouse and the youth reformatory.

Above right: Instead of only minor offenders, everyone from murderers to misdemeanor violators were eventually being incarcerated at Lorton.

Below: Between 1990 and 1994, prisoners attacked Lorton guards nearly 400 times and Lorton was one of the most violent prisons in the country.

Part of the power plant at Lorton.

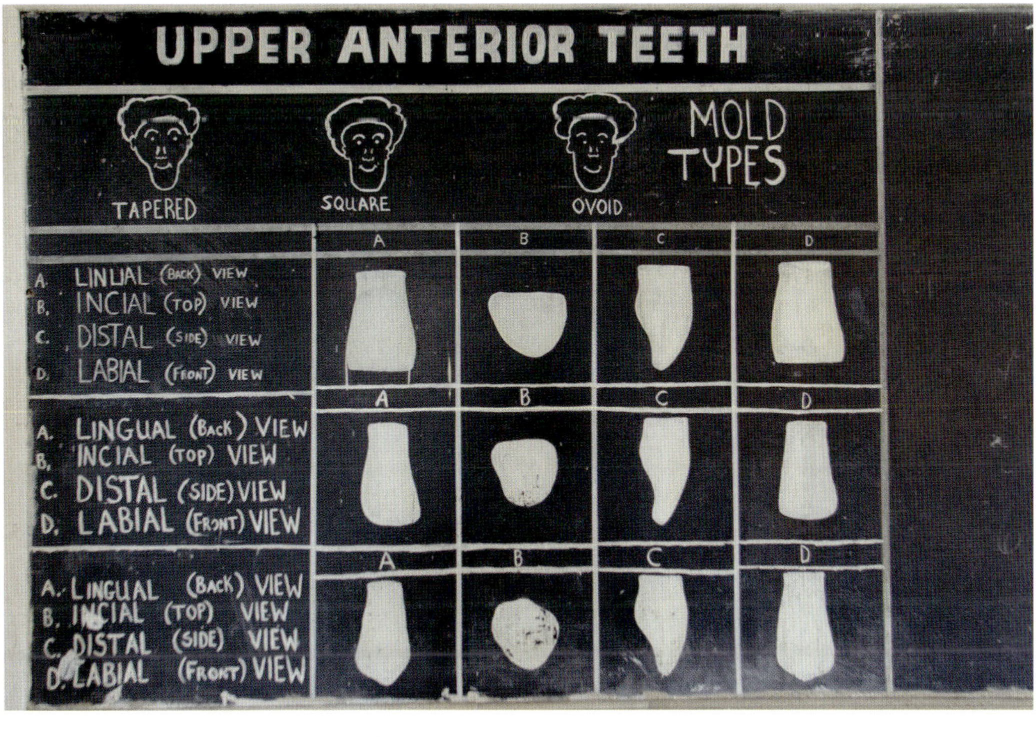

Graphic in the prison's dental services room.

Above left: Norman Mailer, the American novelist and founder of New York's *Village Voice* newspaper, was one of the more notable prisoners at Lorton. Mailer was arrested at an Anti-Vietnam protest. Noam Chomsky, an American linguist and social activist, was also incarcerated at Lorton for Anti-Vietnam demonstrations.

Above right: Other notable inmates include Chuck Brown, musician and considered the father of the Go-Go, 1950; Lucy Burns, suffragist and women's rights advocate, 1917; Alice Paul, suffragist and women's rights activist, and co-founder of the National Woman's Party, 1917; and George Gordon Liddy, FBI agent, talk show host, and burglar of Watergate fame, 1973–1977.

8

LORTON JUVENILE DETENTION CENTER AND NIKE MISSILE SITE

The site of a juvenile detention center was once home to a Cold War missile launch site known as Nike Site W-64. Lorton Juvenile Detention Center in Lorton, VA, was actually part of the Washington, D.C., Department of Corrections and on the same grounds as Lorton Prison. The youth center was built in 1960 near the Nike missile site. It was used for adults between the ages of eighteen and twenty-two to be incarcerated and rehabilitated away from the older, more hardened criminals. The initial concept was that the younger prisoners could acquire a trade and/or get an education and then have their records expunged. The building was designed to resemble the campus of a university, and employed open plan dormitories. Eventually, overcrowding in Lorton Prison forced prison officials to house their inmates at the Youth Center, and it became terribly violent and was soon known as the "murder capital" of the Lorton complex. But by 1997, the Youth Center became a relatively calm and safe place of incarceration again.

This site was also used as one of thirteen in the Washington, D.C./Baltimore area that housed Nike nuclear missiles, and was double the size of the other twelve. Not all of them had actual armed nuclear warheads; this one did: first the Nike-AJAX and then the newer Hercules missiles. These sites were strategic sites maintained between 1954 and 1974 during the Cold War to defend and deter against Soviet missiles. W-64 had a close proximity to Washington, D.C.—about 20 miles—and the Federal Government already owned the land adjacent to Lorton Prison. This site was very obvious and overt, in order to allay fears of nuclear war and was often visited by foreign dignitaries, local politicians, and even residents. When ICBMs and newer technology made the missiles obsolete, the site was decommissioned. All the above ground buildings were razed and the missile launchers were secured and welded shut. The warheads were all removed.

In 1985, a new minimum-security prison was erected on the missile site. The Youth Center complex closed in January 2000; the site is currently being used for fire training and has also been used by the Virginia Task Force One Urban Search and Rescue Team for training.

Above left: Overcrowding in the Lorton Reformatory forced prison officials to house their inmates at the Youth Center, and it became known as the "murder capital" of Lorton.

Above right: One of the youth center buildings housed a Civil Defense Emergency Operations Center bunker operated by the D.C. Office of Emergency Management. Theoretically, the bunker would absorb the shock of a nuclear attack on Washington, D.C.

Below: Cubicles for various agencies were installed so that emergency operations could be conducted from the site in the event of an attack.

Above: The Nike missile site was very obvious and overt, in order to allay fears of nuclear war.

Right: Bored or frustrated prisoners produced a great amount of prison art, some of which is seen here.

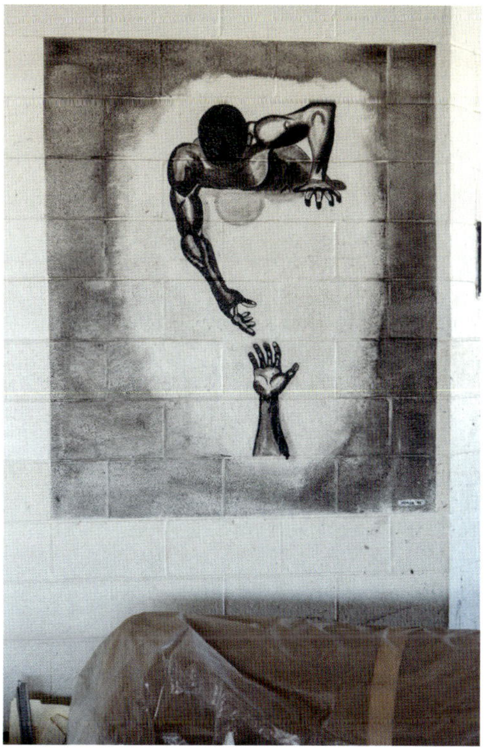

Some of the prisoner art will be on display at the forthcoming Lucy Burns Museum at the Workhouse Arts Center.

9

SWANNANOA

Sub-freezing temperatures in April could not stop us from going to see this majestic fifty-two-room, 23,000-square-foot mansion atop of Afton Mountain in central Virginia. Swannanoa was the summer home of Major James Dooley, a railroad magnate, and his wife, Sallie May. Built in 1912, Dooley used the same architect (Baskervill) that designed Selma Mansion, and one can see the resemblances between Swannanoa and Selma. The Dooley's main home in Richmond, named Maymont, was smaller, and despite Swannanoa's beauty and lavishness, the summer palace was only used by the Dooleys for a few summers before their deaths—James Dooley in 1922 and Sallie three years later.

After the Dooleys' deaths, Swannanoa became a country club and was visited by President Calvin Coolidge, some say due to the excellent moonshine produced there during Prohibition. In 1932, when the country club closed due to the Depression, Swannanoa went unused for seventeen years, until, finally, artists Walter and Lao Russell signed a fifty-year lease with the owner, Alvin Tandy Dulaney of the Skyline Swannanoa Corporation. The couple was never fortunate enough to purchase the property. The Russells created the University of Science and Philosophy (USP) in 1950. The basis of the university was cosmic consciousness and universal light. USP still exists today as home-study courses. Walter Russell died at Swannanoa on his ninety-second birthday. Swannanoa Palace has been registered with both the U.S. National Register of Historic Places and the Virginia Landmarks Register since 1968.

Of course, conspiracy theories abound, as with any old, beautiful, and famous place. Many say the palace is haunted. Some say Swannanoa is a vortex, or an intersection of natural energy, which was reportedly why the USP was located there. One theory says that Swannanoa was the meeting place of the Group or Council of Thirty—a group similar the Illuminati—that has ordered assassinations and incited wars. A couple that lives nearby claims that the Royal Family owns Swannanoa and that they had seen Ted Kennedy and Jackie O., the Queen of England, Henry Kissinger, Spiro Agnew, Gerald Ford, Pope John Paul II, and Margaret Thatcher, among others, drive by on Route 250 heading to the palace.

Swannanoa changed hands again in 1998, and James and Sandi Dulaney, who acquired the mansion and 750 acres from Dulaney's grandfather, Alvin, put more than $3 million into the renovation and restoration of Swannanoa. They attempted to live there, but the upkeep proved to be too much for one couple. Not much has been done since around 2001, and the mansion is starting to show signs of wear again. Miraculously, still intact is the 4,000-piece 10-foot × 12-foot Tiffany glass window that Sallie is the subject of. (The Dulaneys installed bulletproof glass to shield it.)

While the fate of Swannanoa is unknown, the Dulaneys continue to care for the property, and tours are offered in the warmer months.

Swannanoa is a palace built in the Italian Renaissance Revival style. Millionaire James Dooley had it built for his wife, Sallie May. Construction began in 1912. The exterior was completed in 1913 and another eight years were spent on the interior.

Above left: A very detailed marble fireplace is decorated with two cherubs. The gold wallpaper is silk cloth.

Above right: Many of the fixtures at Swannanoa were made of gold or gold-plated. Seen here is the "Persian Room."

Swannanoa Palace boasts fifty-two rooms.

The palace had its own power plant for electricity, and was the first house in the county to have such a luxury. An elevator and a dumbwaiter rounded out the list of such posh fixtures.

A 4,000-piece Tiffany window bearing the likeness of Mrs. Dooley graces the foyer along with a domed ceiling painted with cherubs.

The window cost $100,000 to make in 1912 and is the largest Tiffany installation in a home in the United States.

Painted on the wall in the foyer to the right of the Tiffany window is this English crest; on the opposite wall is the state seal of Virginia.

Detail of the domed ceiling in the foyer of Swannanoa.

Above: Detail of the ceiling and Art Deco-style lighting in the dining room.

Right: Trees now choke the watchtower that stands in the back of the palace.

Above: Swannanoa was designed after the Medici family palace in Italy. The marble used on the exterior of the mansion was sourced from Georgia.

Left: This pergola, part of the terraced gardens, spans the width of the house.

Part of the terraced gardens features a fountain made of marble.

Nestled in the Blue Ridge Mountains, the palace boasts terraced gardens and 590 acres of land in Afton, Virginia.

It took 300 artisans—woodworkers, stone-cutters, leatherworkers, plasterers, upholsterers, etc.—eight years to finish the interior of Swannanoa Palace.

Detail of one of the hand-carved door panels.

Sallie May Dooley may have named the palace Swannanoa because of the abundance of the animals on the property. She also loved the fact that swans mated for life.

The grand staircase is white Carrara marble, chosen by Mr. Dooley himself and then imported from Northern Italy.

10

TRUCK FARM

Between Richmond and Charlottesville lie several acres of grassland that houses an odd menagerie of relics: old, decrepit, rusting, and decaying trucks. Among urban explorers and photographers, it is known simply as 'the truck farm'. Appealing to truck enthusiasts as well as those more visually oriented, the truck farm is a wonder to behold. There are dozens of trucks of all kinds, colors, and vintages: Mack trucks, Ford trucks, White trucks, Fruehauf, Diamond T, Autocar—all crusty and peeling, posing and ready to photograph.

Every kind of truck imaginable exists here: there are several vintage firetrucks, milk delivery vehicles, 1930s era gasoline trucks, diesel trucks, bakery delivery trucks, heavy duty trucks, and pickups. Most of the trucks here date between the 1920s to the 1970s.

Percy L. Duncan ("P. L.") collected these trucks over the course of many years. He was the second generation of truck collectors in his family, so obviously the family has been collecting for a very long time. Photographers were always welcome; admittance was just a phone call away. More trucks in the barns. Do not miss the ones in the woods over there. Stay until dark and light paint the trucks. Mr. Duncan and his sons were always most accommodating and friendly.

Mr. Duncan passed away in 2017, and it is unclear what will become of this remarkable collection. If you go, note that most of the vehicles are on a working farm with cows, so watch where you step. The hood ornaments alone are worth the trip.

Detail of a Big Job fire truck from the Burrowsville Volunteer Fire Department.

The Big Job was a fire truck made by Ford. The F750 came in two engines, the 175-hp engine and the 186-hp engine. The F750 is a conventional-looking cab and C750 was the designation for a cab over the engine with a stubby-looking front end.

Above left: Detail of a Ford Big Job fire truck from the Burrowsville Volunteer Fire Department.

Above right: Detail of a Ford fire truck from the Burrowsville Volunteer Fire Department.

Below: Fall at the Truck Farm is always the best season to photograph, as the colors can rival New England. There are dozens of trucks parked in different configurations around the field that they share with cows

A Ford truck is housed in one of the barns.

A Ford V8, a Ford fire truck, and a truck from Powell's Lumber share the limited interior space.

The Diamond T Motor Car Company was founded in Chicago in 1905 by C. A. Tilt. After making touring cars, the company later became known for trucks. By 1967, as a subsidiary of White Motor Company, it merged with Reo Motor Company and became Diamond Reo Trucks, Inc. During World War II, they produced a heavy truck, which was commandeered by Britain as a tank transporter tractor. Diamond T manufactured two pickup trucks: the Model 80 and the Model 201. Both pickups were powered by the Hercules QX-series 6-cylinder engines. The Model 201 was produced from 1938 to 1949.

The Autocar Company is based in Hagerstown, Indiana. Started in 1897 in Pittsburgh, Pennsylvania, as a manufacturer of Brass era automobiles (automobiles that were named for the prominent brass fittings made between 1896 and 1915, when cars were referred to as "Horseless Carriages") and trucks from 1899, Autocar is the oldest surviving motor vehicle brand in the Western Hemisphere. The last cars were produced in 1911 and the company continued as a maker of severe-duty trucks. The Autocar Company went through many takeovers and now builds three models of custom-engineered, heavy-duty trucks.

A delivery van used by Virginia Dairy was light-painted at night.

The Mack A-30, a medium-duty truck, was produced between 1950 and 1953. Mack trucks are a subsidiary of Volvo.

Several Mack trucks, including a diesel and a thermodyne reside at the truck farm. These engines are from the 1950s and 1960s. Thermodyne engines provided simple, dependable power for a new generation of post-war trucks in a rapidly growing country. Horsepower ranged from 170 to 250. Speed was not something that was sought after yet, since interstates were new and still being built. Moving the loads was the main mission, and Mack delivered again and again.

This detail of an old truck is reminiscent of an old farm and farmhouse.

Above left: Originally a flat emblem, the Mack truck hood ornament will be 100 years old in 2021, and is known as "Mack the Bulldog." The Mack AC truck was strong and tenacious, much like an English bulldog, and the shape of its hood resembled the animal as well. The three-dimensional bulldog was first a decorative radiator cap, but as truck design evolved and the radiator access was moved into the interior of the truck, it became an ornament and handle for windshield washers.

Above right: Detail of a signal light on a truck used by Windsor Trucking Corporation in Reading, Pennsylvania. Manufactured by White Motor Company.

Below: White Motor Company truck with "Super Power" designation. The Cleveland-based White Motor Company manufactured, trucks, busses, and tractors from 1900 until 1980. In the early days, they also made sewing machines and bicycles. In 1980, the company declared bankruptcy and was sold to Volvo, which kept the White name until the late 1990s.

Right: A tree grows through the smokestack of this truck, demonstrating how long this truck has been here.

Below: This colorful truck is a Load-Booster F8 manufactured by Ford between 1948 and 1952.

Above: Detail of the interior of a White truck.

Left: Truck used by Powhatan Motor Co. Lowery Bros. Wrecker Service.

Truck used by Lipton's Pleasant View Farm, Somers, Conn.

Trucks at The Truck Farm appear to be randomly strewn about, however, they are actually put in orderly rows in the field according to a plan that perhaps only Mr. Duncan was aware of.

This truck has resided at the truck farm so long that plants are growing up through the chassis.

The Mack B series was a line of heavy trucks produced by Mack Trucks between 1953 and 1966, and many are still on the road. They were available in a variety of configurations, including as firetrucks and school buses.

11

VIRGINIA ELECTRIC AND POWER COMPANY

> *By the time I was four, I would walk around the corner and wait at a local streetcar stop, get on the streetcar with somebody who looked like they could be my mother and go to the end of the line.*
>
> Maureen Forrester
> Canadian operatic contralto, 1930–2010

At one time, Richmond had streetcars. Richmond was the first city in the nation to have streetcars. A company called the Virginia Railway and Power Company (VR&P) electrified the streetcars. Before too long, there were competing streetcar companies, each with different tracks in downtown Richmond. Eventually, the Richmond Passenger and Power Company was established to bring all the entities together and establish power plants. The streetcars ran until 1949, when buses started to appear *en masse*.

The original Virginia Railway and Power Company, organized in 1909, also supplied local businesses and residents with electricity. It is now known as Dominion Energy and is one of the largest power companies in the nation.

Dominion Energy began as a railroad and streetcar company in the early 1900s, and was known as the Virginia Railway and Power Company.

Dominion Energy had a hydroelectric power plant in Fredericksburg called the Liberty Power Station. The station is located on the Rappahannock River and has been abandoned for more than fifty years.

Above left: There are plans in the works to make the power station a restaurant.

Above right: The dam on the Rappahannock River was built in 1909; mills of all sorts began to appear up and down the river.

Below: The water came into these storage units and was forced into turbines, which turned dynamos. In 1926, the plant was sold to VEPCO (Virginia Electric Power Company), and served mainly as a backup station. In the late 1960s, VEPCO stopped running the plant, as the Rappahannock was too low most of the year to run the turbines.

BIBLIOGRAPHY

Brown, P. L., "Ghost Houses Reflect Fading of Farm Life," *The New York Times*, April 2, 1992, www.nytimes.com/1992/04/02/us/ghost-houses-reflect-fading-of-farm-life.html.

Clifton, I., "Former Prison Youth Center Fills Fire Department Training Needs," *Lorton, VA Patch*, August 2011, www.patch.com/virginia/lorton/former-prison-youth-center-fills-fire-department-training-needs.

Crrlcontributor. "Walk Through History … Mill Sites and Water Power," *Central Rappahannock Regional Library,* October 3, 2018, www.librarypoint.org/blogs/post/mill-sites-and-water-power.

"D.C. Department of Corrections Facility at Lorton Prison Complex Time Line," *Workhouse Prison Museum*, www.workhousemuseums.org/history/d-c-department-of-corrections-facility-at-lorton-prison-complex-time-line.

Dean, E., "Maximum Insecurity," *Washington City Paper*, June 16, 1997, www.washingtoncitypaper.com/news/article/13013216/maximum-insecurity.

Ferranti, S. F., "Gorilla Convict: The Prison Writings of Seth Ferranti: Supermax," *Gangsters Inc.* January 19, 2013, www.gangstersinc.ning.com/profiles/blogs/the-prison-writings-of-seth-ferranti-supermax.

"Foamhenge, Centreville, Virginia," *RoadsideAmerica.com*, www.roadsideamerica.com/story/9209.

"Hans Adam RADER (1706–1773) and Anna Bender PAINTER (1708–1773)," *LPD Press & Rio Grande Books*, nmsantos.com/Tangled-Branches/HansAdamRADER/HansAdamRADER.html.

Harris, H., "The History of a Hauntingly Beautiful House," *The Daily Progress*, May 8, 2013, www.dailyprogress.com/ruralvirginian/news/features/the-history-of-a-hauntingly-beautiful-house/article_7fdc4a1c-b666-11e2-8101-001a4bcf6878.html.

"History," Dominion Energy, www.dominionenergy.com/company/history.

"History of Selma Mansion," Selma Mansion, selmamansionrebirth.com/history-of-selma.

"History of the Gap," Chapman Mill Historic Site, www.chapmansmill.org.

Jentsch, S., "Woodbridge, VA: Lazy Susan Dinner Theater Closed," *The BigScreen Cinema Guide*, October 18, 2013, www.bigscreen.com/j/Woodbridge-VA-Lazy-Susan-Dinner-Theater-Closed/3957.

"Lazy Susan Dinner Theatre," Facebook, www.facebook.com/OfficialLazySusanDinnerTheatrePage.

"Lorton Nike Missile Site E-97," Marker History, www.markerhistory.com/lorton-nike-missile-site-marker-e-97/.

Martinez, R., "Historic Culpeper Church To Be Featured On Paranormal TV Show," *Centreville, VA Patch*, Patch, December 25, 2018, patch.com/virginia/centreville/historic-culpeper-church-be-featured-paranormal-tv-show.

McGreal, C., "How America's Food Giants Swallowed the Family Farms," *The Guardian*, March 9, 2019, www.theguardian.com/environment/2019/mar/09/american-food-giants-swallow-the-family-farms-iowa.

Mckenna, M., "Fixing Fleetwood: One Man's Mission to Restore Iconic Church in Brandy Station," *Exponent*, August 22, 2017, www.starexponent.com/news/fixing-fleetwood-one-man-s-mission-to-restore-iconic-church/article_15261ad3-d6c6-5137-95fe-2747a971dd2b.html.

Montgomery, W. E., *African American Churches in Virginia (1865–1900)*, www.encyclopediavirginia.org/African_American_Churches_in_Virginia_1865-1900#start_entry.

Morton, M., "Saving Selma: Historic Manor Poised for Rebirth After Purchase," *Loudoun Now*, March 17, 2016, loudounnow.com/2016/03/17/saving-selma-historic-manor-poised-for-rebirth-after-purchase/.

"Mr. P.L. Duncan Has Passed," BigMackTrucks.com, February 16, 2017, www.bigmacktrucks.com/topic/48735-mr-pl-duncan-has-passed.

Ockedahl, C., "The Story Behind Mack Trucks' Trademark Bulldog Hood Ornament," Trucks.com, April 8, 2016, www.trucks.com.

Oldenburg, D., The Washington Post, "Conspiracies Lurking Everywhere: Culture: The Tendency to Suspect Unseen Schemes at Work Isn't Solely a Proclivity of Crackpots and Paranoids. Experts Say We're All Susceptible," *Los Angeles Times*, February 9, 1992, www.latimes.com/archives/la-xpm-1992-02-09-vw-3461-story.html.

Olmstead, G., "Down on the Farm," *National Review*, August 15, 2016, www.nationalreview.com/2016/08/small-farms-big-business-family-farms-struggle-against-industrial-agriculture.

Peters, L., "Spooky Swannanoa: Marble Mansion Awaits next Life," *The News*

Leader, September 25, 2015, www.newsleader.com/story/news/local/2015/09/24/swannanoa-future-creepy-mansion-mountain-afton/72734062.

Rader, K. W., "The Rader Church in Timberville, Virginia," *The Rader Family Treehouse*, January 12, 2009, raderfamilytreehouse.blogspot.com/2009/01/rader-church-in-timberville-virginia.html.

"Religion in Early Virginia," The Colonial Williamsburg Official History & Citizenship Site, www.history.org/Almanack/life/religion/religionva.cfm.

"Religion in Virginia," VirginiaPlaces.org, www.virginiaplaces.org/religion/.

Roll, L., "Interview with Anonymous Regarding Ghosts in Selma Mansion," February 3, 2019.

"Selma Mansion Rebirth," Facebook, www.facebook.com/SelmaMansionRebirth2.

Shore, A., "Why Do Properties Become Abandoned," Dronegenuity, October 20, 2018, www.dronegenuity.com/why-properties-become-abandoned.

Soergel, A., "Family Farms Pushed to Get Big or Go Bust," *U.S. News & World Report*, April 4, 2018, www.usnews.com/news/best-states/articles/2018-04-04/family-farms-pushed-to-get-big-or-go-bust.

Strock, A., "Nature Is Reclaiming This One Abandoned Virginia Spot And It's Actually Amazing," OnlyInYourState, January 26, 2016, www.onlyinyourstate.com/virginia/selma-abandoned-va.

Strock, A., "This Abandoned Prison In Virginia Has Dark Secrets That'll Make Your Skin Crawl," OnlyInYourState, November 15, 2017, www.onlyinyourstate.com/virginia/abandoned-lorton-reformatory-va.

"Supper Clubs: A Surviving Phenomenon," Table Agent, tableagent.com/article/supper-clubs-a-surviving-phenomenon.

"Swannanoa: Deconstructing an American Palace," Sometimes Interesting, September 19, 2017, sometimes-interesting.com/2016/08/02/swannanoa-deconstructing-an-american-palace.

Tang, J., "The Old Lorton, Virginia Prison Is Being Turned into Homes. Here's Its Fascinating Story," *Greater Greater Washington*, Sept ember 21, 2018, ggwash.org/view/69004/this-old-lorton-virginia-prison-has-now-become-housing.

"The Impact of the Civil War on John Chapman—Part 3," Milling Minutes, July 23, 2015, millingminutes.wordpress.com/2015/07/23/the-impact-of-the-civil-war-on-john-chapman-part-3.

"Thermodyne And Maxidyne?" BigMackTrucks.com, October 24, 2009, www.bigmacktrucks.com/topic/11168-thermodyne-and-maxidyne.

Trifiletti, C., "Inside Homes: Reinventing Selma," *Washington Life Magazine*, July 14, 2019, washingtonlife.com/2019/07/14/inside-homes-reinventing-selma/.

Vicinanzo, A., "Fredericksburg Power Plant Putting on a Major Light Show Friday

Night," *The Freelance-Star*, September 7, 2017, www.fredericksburg.com/business/local_business/fredericksburg-power-plant-putting-on-major-light-show-friday-night/article_35d29fb9-eb1f-5f2b-9b7a-b2a83a8f3e5d.html.

Weinraub, L. K., "Neighborhood Bites: Lazy Susan Dinner Theatre," *Lorton, VA Patch*, May 26, 2011, patch.com/virginia/lorton/neighborhood-bites-lazy-susan-dinner-theatre.

Wells, K., "Family Works to Preserve and Restore Historic Church in White Post," LocalDMV.com, July 31, 2017, www.localdvm.com/news/virginia/family-works-to-preserve-and-restore-historic-church-in-white-post/778804276.

"Who Are the Primitive Baptists, and What Do They Believe?" GotQuestions.org, February 10, 2010, www.gotquestions.org/Primitive-Baptists.html.

Will, E. H., *The Past-Interesting The Present-Intriguing The Future-Bright A Story of Virginia Electric and Power Company* (New York: The Newcomen Society in North America, 1965).

Williams, S. B., "Alberene Soapstone Company," *Slippery Rock Gazette*, www.slipperyrockgazette.net.

ABOUT THE AUTHOR

Liz Roll is a freelance visual solutions provider, storyteller, and photographer in the Washington, D.C./Northern Virginia area. Liz began her career at the American Red Cross as a photographer and eventually moved over to FEMA, the Federal Emergency Management Agency, where she has documented dozens of natural disasters, including Hurricanes Katrina and Sandy. She also does historical documentation (i.e. urban blight) photography, documentary videos, events, conferences, and magazine shoots. Liz photographed many VIPs, including four presidents, three vice-presidents, and others too numerous to count. Liz is an adrenaline junkie.